HORRIBLE
HANK

Written by John Parker
Illustrated by Brent Chambers

04 03 02 01 00
11 10 9 8 7 6 5

Published by Shortland Publications Inc.

Distributed in the United States of America by

a division of Reed Elsevier Inc.
500 Coventry Lane
Crystal Lake, IL 60014
800-822-8661

Printed through Bookbuilders, Hong Kong.

ISBN: 0-7901-0983-2

HORRIBLE
HANK

Written by John Parker
Illustrated by Brent Chambers

This is a pair of thigh-high leather pirate boots.

This is a cutlass (rather rusty).

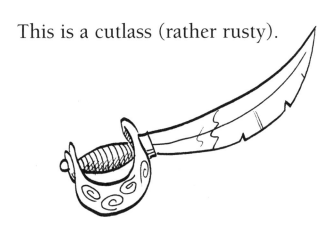

Add one pistol,

one leather belt,

one pirate hat,

plus a parrot,
and you have...

Horrible Hank – the evilest pirate in the whole of the seven seas!

Oops! Let's do that again.
Much better! (And much more evil.)

The trouble was, Horrible Hank wasn't very evil at all. He took up pirating as a promise to his extremely evil father – Hideous Hal – to follow in the family trade.

PROMISE ME, MY BOY, THAT WHEN I'M GONE YOU'LL TAKE UP PIRACY. LOOT! ROB! PILLAGE! STEAL! MAKE THEM WALK THE PLANK IN SHARK-INFESTED SEAS! BE MEAN, NASTY, DISGUSTING, GRUESOME, GRIM, GRISLY, AND GHASTLY – THAT'S A GOOD BOY!

OK, DAD.

9

So Horrible Hank (his father gave him the name) sailed forth in the *Smash'n'Grab* in search of treasure!

Here's the crew.

FOURFINGERS

BUNGEYE

STEWPOT
(COOK)

STEWPOT'S SOUP
OF THE DAY

Cockroach Chowder
* Weevils
* Worms
* Rotten Cabbage
* Cockroaches
* The odd slug
or two...
(Plus an even
slug)
You'll luv love it

The seas sparkled so much that Horrible Hank felt good. But this was a worry – after all, he was supposed to be nasty.

THEN!

(AND PLAIN BAD LUCK)

It so happened that Horrible Hank was up in the crow's nest, looking for galleons, when a passing sea gull bumped into him and somehow flew off with his glasses!

As we might have said, it was pretty bad luck – for both.

BUT...

GOOD NEWS!

The glasses fell off the sea gull.

BAD NEWS!

They fell – plonk! – into the mysterious, unfathomable, unplumbed, deep, dark, lonely* depths of the sea.

* Author's Note: *Sorry about all these adjectives. I'm trying to say that the glasses are lost – forever!*

Horrible Hank felt miserable, even when Polly tried to cheer him up.

HEAR THE ONE ABOUT THE WHALE AND THE SARDINE?

WOLLY CRANTS A PACKER!

After all, without his glasses, he couldn't see straight. Everything was a blur. This is what Horrible Hank's map looked like when he read it with his glasses on...

MAP — given to Horrible Hank by Hideous Hal

Seatown
(watch out for
dungeon &
Judge Scrimshaw)

Ye High Cliffs

Secret Caves
for Hiding Treasure

SCALE
←10 MILES→

This is what the map looked like *without* glasses –

like a foggy day in the middle of an earthquake.

And without glasses, Horrible Hank even had trouble seeing his crew.

Still, Horrible Hank tried bravely to do his best.

MUST BE GRISLY AND GRUESOME. SNARL! SNAP! ARRGH!

WHERE AM I?

One day, Fourfingers spied a ship on the horizon.

AHOY, SKIPPER! THERE'S A SHIP THREE POINTS ON THE PORT BOW! 'TIS THE *FAIR ROSE*, A RICH GALLEON. DOUBLOONS, PIECES OF EIGHT, RUBIES, RICHES, GREED!

Up went the Jolly Roger pirate flag,

while the crew all prepared a fearsome array of weapons...

CUTLASSES

DAGGERS

HEADSCRATCHERS

PISTOLS

POLLY WANTS A PISTOL, TOO!

KNUCKLE SANDWICHES

AXES

plus terrifying expressions (facial),

and terrifying expressions (vocal).

But what good are terrifying expressions (vocal and facial) when the captain can't see straight?

Just for starters, when Horrible Hank threw out the grappling irons, they were supposed to catch the *Fair Rose*. Instead, they entangled him and his crew.

Horrible Hank tried again. Untangling himself with a superhuman effort, he made a huge leap to the *Fair Rose.*

Author's Note:

Ready for a simple problem? When the distance between Object A and Object B is 10 feet, what is the noise made by Object C, traveling between A and B, if Object C travels only 9 feet?

FOR THE ANSWER, TURN TO THE NEXT PAGE

To save further embarrassment, let us draw a curtain over Horrible Hank's attempts.

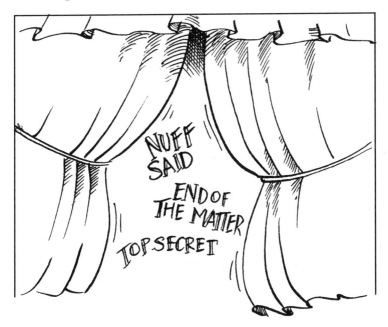

We'll just say that he made such a mess of it that Fourfingers, Bungeye, and Stewpot decided to lie down in their hammocks with headaches.

And when Stewpot tried to cheer them up at the end of the day with his Soup of the Day... well...

Everyone got a stomachache, too.

The next day, the crew told Horrible Hank he just *had* to have glasses.

Stewpot's suggestion sounded sensible enough – BUT...

BIG PROBLEM!!

In Seatown resided the dreaded Judge Scrimshaw.

Whenever a pirate was brought before him for sentencing, he threw the book at him.

To show you what I mean, here's page one of Judge Scrimshaw's punishment book.

Name	Crime	Punishment
SKINFLINT SID	Not paying his grocer's bill	Rats for breakfast (raw)
ROUND ROGER	Overeating and throwing his weight around	Four thousand push-ups daily
JINKY JACK	Running away from Seatown Jail	Hang by fingernails in snake-infested dungeon
PEGLEG PETE	Tripping while dancing the hornpipe	Pelt with Mrs. Scrimshaw's rock cakes.

Nasty, eh?

So, no wonder Horrible Hank didn't fancy going to Seatown for a pair of specs.

But if he didn't get glasses, then the crew of the *Smash'n'Grab* was likely to catch nothing but seaweed and colds.

It was a

And soon there was a

The *Smash'n'Grab* ran aground!!!

You see, Horrible Hank and his crew were so busy discussing the glasses problem that they failed to keep a sharp and proper lookout. So they didn't notice a small island sneaking up to starboard.

AUTHOR'S NOTE:
Failing to keep a sharp and proper lookout can happen to all of us. Just the other day, I was putting away the dishes in the bottom cupboard, having forgotten I'd opened the door of the top cupboard.

So when I stood up – WHAMMO!!!!!! It's the first time I've seen stars in the daylight!

Anyway, on with the story.

Whales

Whale

Whir...

Rocks
they
luckily
missed

Beach

Island

Smash 'n' Grab

Dolphins gamboling

All the pirates, of course, got a terrible
shock, especially when a clear voice
rang out.

And, nimbly scaling up the sides,
appeared...

Henrietta!!

How did she land on the island? Why was she there? Who was she, anyway?

For her story, read on.

Henrietta's Story

Hello, shipmates! My name is Henrietta. I was the chief cook on the *Fair Rose, until* yesterday, when the *Smash'n'Grab tried to* board us.

When the silly pirate on that boat got into such a fix with his grappling irons, I giggled fit to bust!

And when he tried to leap aboard and fell into the sea, I laughed so much that I, too, fell overboard.

So I swam to this island with nothing to my name but the clothes I wear, a hungry stomach, and a pair of rusty glasses I found washed up on the beach.

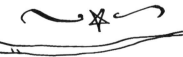

Now, back to the action.

Henrietta held a pair
of glasses that looked
like this:

Horrible Hank saw them
more like this:

But he still yelled out loud and clear –

GIVE ME MY GLASSES,
OR YOU'LL WALK THE
PLANK!!!

But Henrietta wasn't bothered at all.

And she sprang like a cat into the rigging, climbing like a monkey up the tallest mast.

She tied the glasses to the very top of that tallest mast, and then swung dizzily down to stand on the deck again.

Now, climbing up to the top of the highest mast isn't everyone's cup of tea (especially if you drink only orange juice)...

so **HORRIBLE HANK** felt quite giddy...

FOURFINGERS and **BUNGEYE** got headaches again...

and **STEWPOT** decided to cook another Soup of the Day to cheer everyone up.

Another Soup of the Day. That was bad news!!

BUT WORSE WAS TO

FOLLOW!!

PREPARE FOR AN

ANNOUNCEMENT

BY HENRIETTA

THE GLASSES ARE YOURS, HORRIBLE HANK, ONLY AFTER YOU'VE SAILED INTO THE PORT OF SEATOWN AND MENDED YOUR EVIL PIRATE WAYS!!

Horrible Hank rolled his eyes in despair. To go to Seatown and face Judge Scrimshaw! In desperation, he tried to pull out his beard, but, fortunately just in time, realized he hadn't grown one.

But there was nothing they could do. So when the *Smash'n'Grab* floated off the beach at the next high tide, back to Seatown they sailed.

At least their voyage home was cheered up by Henrietta's wonderful cooking.

Out of:
- scraps of stale salt beef
- weevily crackers
- moldy bread
- barnacles
- and a flying fish or two...

she made the most delicious, delectable, scrumptious, mouth-watering, stomach-satisfying, nose-tingling feast of Henrietta-heavenly delights!!!

When they reached Seatown, Henrietta climbed up the mast again and gave the glasses to Horrible Hank.

He dropped them on his nose with a huge sigh of relief, but...

This is what Seatown looked like.

In other words, the glasses belonged to someone else!

Then to make matters worse, Horrible Hank and his caustic crew were marched off to the courthouse.

And to add to Horrible Hank's misery, Judge Scrimshaw was in a terrible mood. (Mrs. Scrimshaw had just baked some rock cakes.)

Things looked ██████ for Horrible Hank... until Henrietta rose to speak in his defense.

55

The court (and Judge Scrimshaw) were saddened by the tale.

The court was startled when Judge Scrimshaw leaped to his feet.

He ran toward Horrible Hank and stared at the glasses.

Those glasses were his!

BLESS MY SOUL! THE VERY GLASSES I LOST FORTY-ONE YEARS AGO WHILE ON AN ISLAND PICNIC! MY DEAR DEPARTED MOTHER GAVE THEM TO ME.

OH HAPPY DAY!

So a happy Judge Scrimshaw let them go free, on the condition they give up piracy and live by an honest trade. But what could they do?

AUTHOR'S NOTE: *Perhaps* **you** *can supply the answer. Think about it...*

Horrible – sorry – Happy Hank had a crew and a boat. Henrietta was a wonderful cook. One ship and a crew and a cook. Put them all together and you have a...

FLOATING
RESTAURANT!

BETTER THAN PIRACY TEE-HEE!

The restaurant was an amazing success. Henrietta cooked, with help from Stewpot in everything – *except* Soup of the Day.

Fourfingers and Bungeye waited on the tables, and Happy Hank took the money.

Here's a sample menu.

MENU

Henrietta's Stewpot

Chops à la cutlass

Walk-the-Plank Steak

Hidden Treasure Dessert

Of course, Happy Hank bought himself a pair of gold-rimmed glasses from the best spectacle-maker in town.

When he put them on and saw Henrietta sharp and clear for the first time – well! They got married the very same day!

TITLES IN THE SERIES

SET 9A

Television Drama
Time for Sale
The Shady Deal
The Loch Ness Monster Mystery
Secrets of the Desert

SET 9B

To JJ From CC
Pandora's Box
The Birthday Disaster
The Song of the Mantis
Helping the Hoiho

SET 9C

Glumly
Rupert and the Griffin
The Tree, the Trunk, and the Tuba
Errol the Peril
Cassidy's Magic

SET 9D

Barney
Get a Grip, Pip!
Casey's Case
Dear Future
Strange Meetings

SET 10A

A Battle of Words
The Rainbow Solution
Fortune's Friend
Eureka
It's a Frog's Life

SET 10B

The Cat Burglar of Pethaven Drive
The Matchbox
In Search of the Great Bears
Many Happy Returns
Spider Relatives

SET 10C

Horrible Hank
Brian's Brilliant Career
Ferntickles
It's All in Your Mind,
James Robert
Wing High, Gooftah

SET 10D

The Week of the Jellyhoppers
Timothy Whuffenpuffen-
Whippersnapper
Timedetectors
Ryan's Dog Ringo
The Secret of Kiribu Tapu Lagoon

As for the *Smash'n'Grab*, it got a sparkling coat of paint and varnish. Now it is the finest-looking ship in Seatown.

It's not called the *Smash'n'Grab* anymore. If you're ever in Seatown, look for it under a new name...

THE SMASHING GRUB !!!

THE GRUBBING SMASH! POLLY WANTS TWO CRACKERS!

THE END